Dealing Redemptively

With Those Involved In
Divorce and Remarriage Problems

J. C. Wenger

HERALD PRESS, SCOTTDALE, PA.

DEALING REDEMPTIVELY WITH THOSE INVOLVED IN
DIVORCE AND REMARRIAGE PROBLEMS

This booklet was first printed in 1954 by the
South Central Mennonite Conference,
Hesston, Kansas

Third Printing, 1968

Printed in United States

Cover design by Joseph Alderfer

Foreword

This booklet is an address which the author delivered to the South Central Mennonite Conference in session near Eldon, Mo., August 17-20, 1954. Out of the discussions on the question of divorce at this conference the following action was taken:

In the light of Scriptural teaching on divorce, and in consideration of the devastating effects of this sin on present-day society, and in recognition of the many and varied situations which arise in connection with this problem, be it resolved,

a. That we go on record as standing firmly against the divorce evil.

b. That we emphasize in our teaching program the permanency of the marriage relationship and seek to conserve the spiritual values of homelife.

c. That we endeavor to deal redemptively and in the spirit of Christian love with those who have become involved in this sin.

d. That we approve the attitude expressed by the General Problems Committee of General Conference report, paragraph No. 4, page 82, in General Conference Report, 1953, which reads as follows: "We do recognize that there are many and varied difficult situations in many places in our constituency and also the procedure and requirements have been dealt with in various ways by individual congregations and conferences. We feel that this right should be granted, that it should continue to be the responsibility of the individual conference, congregation, its pastors, teachers, and workers to meet every situation, solving it in the light of Scriptures. The challenge today is for the church to come forward with still renewed vigor, in the power of God, using every means possible to cry out against this evil. We have the press, the radio, the many pulpits, our young people's organizations, our pastors and Christian workers at our disposal to speak forth the message of the Gospel."

Dealing Redemptively with Those Involved in Divorce and Remarriage Problems

Introduction

The church of Christ is called to minister the Word of God, and present the demands of the Gospel for repentance and faith, to a world hopelessly lost in sin. It is the intention of God that all men should be saved by coming to the Lord Jesus Christ, the Saviour and Redeemer. Those who come to Jesus are required and enabled by God to cease from sin and to live holy lives. All manner of sins are forgiven when one repents and believes. Problems arise only when the regenerated seek to disentangle themselves from the sinful involvements which they contracted while still unconverted. So much seems clear from God's Word, and it would seem that we are all able to agree on these general truths.

A particular application of these truths to the situation of the divorced and remarried brings a number of difficult problems to the church. It has long been so. The decision of the Catholic Church, arrived at in the early centuries of this era, is that adultery allows separation from bed and board but never permits the remarriage of either partner as long as the other survives. As long as the Mennonite Church had no divorces of its own, and as long as no mission work was carried on, it was not necessary to face this question. Consequently there was little attention paid to this problem in our brotherhood prior to 1865.

Now we are living in a different era, and we have begun to carry out more earnestly the command of our Saviour to make disciples of all nations. What shall we do about those who are divorced and remarried, and who then find the Saviour?

Let us divide the message into three parts: (1) The Teaching of the Bible on Divorce and Remarriage; (2) Our Struggles with This Problem in the Past Ninety Years; and (3) An Attempt to Arrive at a Solution which would be true to Scripture and yet redemptive for those entangled in divorce and remarriage. We all recognize that this is no easy task. But with souls at stake, are we permitted to shirk such difficult problems? Are not the Spirit and the Word able to lead us in this as well as other matters? God give us the humility and open-mindedness necessary to discern His blessed will!

1. THE TEACHING OF THE BIBLE ON DIVORCE AND REMARRIAGE

1. What Is Marriage?

By marriage we understand the God-established institution of the lifelong union of a man and a woman by mutual agreement and promise, culminating in the sexual union which symbolizes the complete self-giving of each to the other. Marriage was instituted of God at the beginning of the human race, and according to the Mosaic account was intended to be both permanent and monogamous. Our Saviour confirmed this clearly in Matthew 19. Following the fall of Adam and Eve, and the entrance of sin into human nature and life, marriage continued as one of God's good natural blessings even for those who were not of faith. It is not a sin for two unsaved people to get married. The sin consists in refusing to repent and believe. In the widest sense, marriage is therefore broader

8

than the church; it includes those non-Christians who have agreed to live together and thus to establish homes. There is no Scriptural warrant for calling the marriages of unsaved people adulterous, or for granting them the right to separate at will.

2. Divorce and Remarriage in the Old Testament

If we want to know God's will for marriage we may consult Genesis 1 and 2, and the New Testament commentaries on those passages. If we want to study divorce, however, we must turn to Deuteronomy 24. The best Hebrew scholars tell us that the rendering of the first four verses of this chapter in our common English version is not quite exact. The Hebrew is not saying that it is the will of God for a man to divorce the wife in whom he finds something offensive, as verse 1 of the King James Version would indicate. Rather, the Hebrew runs the *if* clauses down to the end of verse 3. This means that the passage recognizes that sinful Israel will divorce and remarry. But when that does occur, God is registering His absolute prohibition against resuming the first marriage after a second union has been contracted, regardless of whether the second marriage ends in divorce or by the death of the second husband. The divorced woman or widow may never return to the first husband under any circumstances. In other words, God tolerates divorce in this passage, but does not institute or command it. What God does do, is to forbid the resumption of a union which has been broken by a second marriage. This understanding of the Hebrew is confirmed by the rendering of the Septuagint, the Greek Old Testament, and by the ablest Hebrew scholars, both conservative and liberal. (See the discussion in Professor John Murray's able book, *Divorce*, Philadelphia, 1953, pp. 3-16.)

Thus we see that God gives through Moses the revelation that marriage should be a permanent union of one man and woman, that God tolerated the sinful institution of divorce and remarriage, but strictly limited it by refusing the right to resume a union which has been followed by a second marriage. The prophet Malachi states that the Lord, the God of Israel, hates putting away (Mal. 2:16), confirming the teaching of God through Moses. And Jeremiah (3:1) teaches that the resumption of first marriages, after the contracting of other unions, greatly pollutes the land; once again confirming the legislation given through Moses.

3. Divorce and Remarriage in the Old Testament

When we come to the New Testament we find that our Lord and His apostles once more go back to Genesis to establish on that foundation the will of God that marriage is a union of one man and one woman for life.

In Matthew 19, the Saviour specifically rejected the easy divorce system which the Mosaic law tolerated because of Israel's hardheartedness, and called His followers up to the higher law given by the Creator to Adam and Eve. Mark 10 and Luke 16, as well as Romans 7 and I Corinthians 7, all teach that marriage is permanent, and that divorce is no longer to be allowed. We are no longer living in the days of Deuteronomy 24, as far as God is concerned.

But now a new problem arises. What about the exception clauses in Matthew 5 and 19? While there is a bit of variation in the manuscripts, the fact of the exceptions cannot be denied on textual grounds. It should be noted, however, that just as in Deuteronomy 24, Matthew 5:32 does not report that Jesus commanded or even wished for the putting away of the adulterous companion. The Lord simply said that anyone who puts away his companion

10

makes her an adulteress, likely in the sense that he puts her into a situation in which she will contract a new union with some other man, when as a matter of plain fact her union with the first husband still stands in God's sight. The exception clause, then, is not a divine command to put away the wife. It simply indicates that when a man does dismiss his unfaithful companion he is not guilty of making her an adulteress: she did that herself.

Incidentally, it is not possible to argue from the English word *fornication* that the sin indicated by Matthew in the exception clause had to do with premarital unfaithfulness or unchastity. The word was used of various types of sexual sin on the part of both married and single people. It is used in I Corinthians 5, of the incestuous union of a man with his stepmother, for example.

Does the exception clause of Matthew 19:9 confer on the innocent companion the right to remarry? In the judgment of the Swiss Brethren of the years 1525-30 the answer is in the affirmative. This is in contrast with Roman Catholics, of course, but they are moved by other considerations than Greek syntax: they have a sacramental theory to uphold. As the Catholic scholar, Dr. George D. Smith says "—in one place our Lord appears to allow an exception to an otherwise universal law. For a Catholic, the meaning of Christ's teaching is known, not by wrangling over texts, but by the infallible authority of the church." *(The Teachings of the Catholic Church, Vol. II,* p. 1094). But Protestants have no other recourse than to patiently and carefully examine every relevant passage before making a doctrinal decision on any topic. And in the opinion of the best Greek exegetes the language of Matthew 19:9 implies that the unfaithfulness of one partner releases the other from the marriage bond. The main thrust of Matthew 19:9 is on the sin of remarriage: "Who-

11

ever puts away his wife and marries another is guilty of adultery." The chief sin contemplated here is that involved in the illicit remarriage. To make the exceptive clause apply only to the putting away makes nonsense of the sentence, "Whoever puts away his wife, except for fornication, commits adultery." But that would not be true. It is he who remarries while the first companion lives who is committing adultery. "He who puts away his wife, except for fornication, and marries another, commits adultery." Therefore he who puts away his wife for fornication, and marries another, does not commit adultery. In other words, the sin of contracting a union with someone other than one's spouse is so awful that it has the same effect on the marriage bond as does death. The innocent party may remarry without sin. This is the implication of the grammar. But it should be noted that this conclusion is never explicitly stated anywhere in the New Testament.

Of course, it is also necessary to raise the question: What about the absolute prohibitions of Mark, Luke, and Paul? The only satisfactory answer, in my judgment, is that Mark, Luke, and Paul are giving only the general rule, and that Matthew alone is recording the exception. It is more sound hermeneutically to allow the exception to modify the absolute statements of the other Biblical writers than for the general statements to deny absolutely the truth of Matthew's exceptive clause.

The discussion in I Corinthians 7 seems to indicate the following seven truths: (1) The single state is perfectly pleasing to God, for single people if contented are more free to devote themselves to the Lord's work. (2) To avoid fornication, let each person have a companion. (Is not this relevant for our present problem?) (3) Marriage obligates the partners to enter ungrudgingly into the physical union,

12

so that neither partner may be tempted to sin because of the refusal of the other. (4) Unmarried people and widows may marry if the urge is such as to destroy peace of mind. (5) Where the marriage is sufficiently unhappy as to provoke thoughts of separation, the partners are exhorted to persevere in the union. Yet, if the incompatibility actually drives them apart, they shall remain unmarried or effect a reconciliation. (Please note that nothing is said about adultery here.) (6) If a believer is married to an unbeliever, the believer shall not initiate a separation. But if the unbeliever leaves, let him depart. There is no obligation to attempt to maintain a union against the wishes of the unbelieving companion. (7) Stay in the situation in which you found yourself when you became a believer, whether circumcised, or uncircumcised, slave, freeman, married or single. Three times (verses 17, 20, 24) Paul commands his readers to remain in the situation in which they were when God called them. This was, said he, his rule in all the churches.

It should be noted that in general the New Testament is content to lay down fundamental principles only. It does not attempt to answer every possible question related to marriage and divorce. What should be done if a marriage is contracted with someone who is so physically abnormal as not to be capable of consummating the marriage union? (No answer.) What should be done if one marries, in perfect innocence, a bigamist? (No answer.) What should be done in the case of a heathen polygamist who gets converted? (No answer.) What should be done in the case of a fornicator who lived in sin with someone for a period of time before contracting his present marriage relationship? (No answer.) What shall be done about those who were divorced and remarried before being called into God's kingdom? (No answer.)

Why is there no answer to these situations, dearly beloved? Surely not because God did not think of these possibilities! It must rather be that He intended to allow His church by the leading of the Holy Spirit to seek His will by earnest prayer, and with humble, seeking minds, following the general principles of His Word.

4. Summary

Perhaps it would now be in order to summarize briefly some of the principles observed so far:

1. When a couple marries they are obligated by God's law to remain true to each other for life. Matthew 19:9.

2. When either commits adultery or gets a divorce on grounds other than adultery, he is guilty of sin in God's sight. Luke 19:20; Matthew 5:32.

3. Through Moses and Jeremiah God stated forcibly that remarried people shall never under any circumstances return to the former companion. (This is neither changed nor confirmed in the New Testament.) Deuteronomy 24:4.

4. The law of Moses compelled a fornicator to marry the humiliated girl and gave him no license to put her away all her days. Deuteronomy 22:29. Menno Simons regarded this as still in force. (*Works,* I, 145): "If you would not lose your soul, you will have to marry her and not forsake her." The New Testament neither changes nor confirms this law of Moses.

5. It is a sin to marry a second companion with the first still living, the only possible exception being the innocent party. Matthew 19:9.

6. It is a sin to marry an unbeliever. I Corinthians 7:39.

7. If however one is already married to an unbeliever, he shall not terminate the union. I Corinthians 7:12-16.

8. Converts are to remain in the same social situation as they were in when they were called into the kingdom of Christ. One cannot help wondering whether this was

given three times in the course of a discussion on the married, the single, the quarreling partners, the believer-unbeliever unions, and the problem of the man with a daughter or sweetheart, to give guidance to those many divorced and remarried people in the Graeco-Roman world of the first century, some of whom undoubtedly became Christians. If so, it would be in line with the counsel of Paul to *continue* the believer-unbeliever union though it is a sin to *contract* such a union. It would also be in line with the judgment of Menno Simons that those who had humbled girls before marriage should not now abandon their lawful wives to return to the ruined girl of their premarital days. (*Works, I,* 145.)

9. No one believes that remarriage is the unpardonable sin.

10. In closing this portion of the study we may remark that to seek to redeem those caught in the remarriage sin would not mean the abandonment of our teaching on the duty of husbands and wives to remain true to each other for life. No more so than Paul's allowing the continuance of a union with an unbeliever would weaken his teaching that Christians shall marry only believers.

II. THE STRUGGLE OF THE MENNONITE BROTHERHOOD WITH THE DIVORCE AND REMARRIAGE QUESTION FROM 1865 TO 1945

It should first of all be observed that divorce was quite rare in the first part of the period under consideration. And yet the Mennonite Church faced the question occasionally. In October 1867, one of the questions discussed in the Indiana Conference was whether a remarried man, whose first wife was still living, could be received as a member of the church. It was decided in the negative. The Amish General Conference of the same year took the same position, spelling out its decisions in some detail. The first move in the other direction seems to have been made by the Virginia Conference as early as September 1867. The report of Frederick A. Rhodes which was printed in the *Herald of Truth* the following November states: "It was also decided that for the same reason that a man is allowed to put away his wife he is allowed to marry again." This view was in exact agreement with the ancient Swiss Brethren tract. As was noted above, the Indiana Conference at first took the opposite position. In the January, 1868, issue of the *Herald of Truth,* Editor John F. Funk therefore called for further discussion of the matter in a proper spirit so that "during the next conferences the matter may be properly decided."

One of the strong leaders who complied with Funk's suggestion was Bishop John M. Brenneman (1816-95) of Elida, Ohio, a man who had then been a bishop over twenty-five years. He reported that it was he himself who had brought up the question in the Virginia Conference, and that he had supported the decision of conference to allow the innocent party to remarry. He went on to quote Tertullian and other ancient church fathers, Menno Simons, the old Mennonite catechism, the Shorter Catechism, etc., in support of the Virginia Conference interpretation of Matthew 5:32. He also reported that the decision of the Virginia Conference was adopted unanimously. But the Ohio and Indiana brethren, in their semiannual conferences which alternated between the two states in those days, rejected the Virginia interpretation in both their spring and fall meetings of 1868. Bishop Brenneman also lost his courage and begged for pardon in the July, 1868, *Herald of Truth.* The Amish General Conference of 1870 also reaffirmed its position of 1867 rejecting divorce and remarriage for members of the church.

1. Indiana Conference

But the tide soon turned back in favor of the 1867 Virginia Conference position. The Indiana Mennonite Conference of 1875 discussed the case of a brother who had married a divorced woman. Could he be reinstated as a brother? The conference minutes read as follows: "The fact that he had been a brother, having known the requirement of the Gospel as well as the rules of the church on this point, makes it a very serious transgression. But if he truly repents, and brings forth fruits meet for repentance, he can be received again according to I Corinthians 6:9-11. In reference to this matter, it may be remarked that . . . the woman not being a member of the church, neither her first husband, they were out of Christ and hence under the civil law, and being divorced under that law . . . she under the law was no longer bound to him. And we are taught that upon true repentance, all sin except blasphemy against the Holy Ghost shall be forgiven."

Twelve years later, in 1887, a similar case was considered. A man had married a woman years before who proved unfaithful and whom he divorced. He then married another woman who later died. By the time of the 1887 conference he had not heard of his first wife for ten years, but she had at that time been remarried also. This man now wished to marry a sister in the church and applied for membership himself. The conference minutes read as follows: "Brother Funk stated that it has been decided in the Indiana Conference that when such (people) come in the spirit of true penitence they can be received, provided they have done such act while they were in the world without Christ, and have been divorced from their marriage relations. Brother Nice [Bishop Henry Nice, 1822-92, of Sterling, Illinois] followed with statements [along] the same line. Brother Jos. Holdeman stated that if we stand upon the articles of our confession the matter is clear.

"Remarks were made to show that the church cannot sanction the giving of divorces where Scriptural cause does not exist. The question was also asked whether those who had been married and had separated from their companions without the Scriptural cause, and without a divorce, may be received into membership. Other explanations followed to show that those separate without a divorce, if they will neither seek a divorce nor marry again, may be received into membership. I Corinthians 7:11."

A year later, at the very first session of the Indiana Amish Mennonite Conference, in 1888, it was asked whether a person who had been remarried while a former companion still lived, and having made a profession of faith before such act, could be received into church membership. The minutes record the following: "Majority in favor of taking such a one into the church, but was given into the hands of the Nappanee ministers, it being their case."

2. Lancaster Conference

My own grandfather whose family lived in the Weaverland area of Lancaster County, Pennsylvania, told my father that one of the charges which the Stauffer Mennonites preferred against the Mennonites of the Lancaster Conference was that Bishop George Weaver (uncle of Bishop Benjamin Weaver and of Preacher John W. Weaver), who served as a bishop from 1854 until 1883, tolerated a brother in the church who was "living with another man's wife." The man was evidently married to a divorced woman.

3. Franconia Conference

The Franconia Conference also faced the remarriage problem in the Towamencin congregation, in 1887. The conference decided in the May session of that year that a man married to a divorced woman might be received if the congregation voted unanimously in favor of doing so. Clearly, the only point of concern in the conference was the unity of the church.

The Missouri-Iowa Conference formerly granted one of its mission workers permission to receive into membership penitent converts who were remarried.

It is thus evident that the prevailing view in the Mennonite Church in the latter decades of the nineteenth century was that marriage ought to be permanent. But where lives were broken by sin, and people were divorced and remarried legally, and the Spirit of God then brought them to repentance and faith; our brotherhood then stretched out to them a welcoming hand and received them as members, in spite of the sins of the past. Our church then followed the principle—Whatever one's state was when he was called of God, let him abide in that state. I Corinthians 7:17, 20, 24.

4. After 1900

But once again the tide turned. A new generation of leaders appeared around the turn of the century, men who did much to mold the Mennonite Church into the kind of group it now is. Outstanding among them was our revered Brother Daniel Kauffman. These men began to understand the continuance of a second marriage relation, with a former companion still living, as a continuing sin. (This the Bible never states explicitly, however.) But the view became more and more commonly accepted. In 1905 General Conference went on record as believing that people holding a divorce "obtained for the sake of remarriage, or being married a second time, and continuing to live with the second companion while first companion is living, should not be received into the church."

19

This resolution was endorsed by the Kansas-Nebraska Conference in 1909. In 1903 the Indiana-Michigan Conference ruled that a remarried person could be received into the church fellowship "if the party to whom he or she was first married is dead." The first semiofficial statement that living with a divorced person constitutes a continuing sin of adultery that I could find is in the 1914 *Bible Doctrine,* p. 452: "Therefore whoever lives with wife No. 2 while wife No. 1 is still alive lives in adultery." This view of Brother Daniel Kauffman gained general acceptance in our brotherhood, and is only in recent years being reexamined and questioned.

The problem is this: In a semisecular civilization such as we have in the United States, where many families have no connection with the church, where the Bible is not read in the home, where people work on Sunday, take God's name in vain, and give other evidences of a complete disregard of Christ and the Bible; and where many divorces and remarriages occur: if we are to do mission work with such people, we are forced to at least reconsider a stand which has nothing to offer such remarried people except to tell them to cease living together as husband and wife. We grant that they sinned by divorcing their first companions for largely unworthy reasons. We grant that they committed adultery by remarrying instead of being reconciled to their companions. But the door of reconciliation is often closed by the other partner having also contracted a second marriage. And what about God calling the resumption of such a first union, an "abomination before the Lord," and that which "pollutes" the land? Have these warnings no relevance for us at all? And when Paul interrupts his discussion of marriage three times to say: In whatever state a person was when God called him, let him remain in that state—has that also no relevance at all? And if it is evident that God calls and accepts as sons and daughters those who are remarried, giving them joy and peace, who are we to refuse them admission into the body of Christ?

5. *Personal Judgments*

It is thus already evident that I am inclined to feel that the position of our brotherhood seventy-five years ago was more redemptive and Christian than the later view which displaced it. I hold this position with humility and with some misgivings, but yet with deep conviction. For what are the alternatives? Here are eight alternatives: 1. Tell them to break up their home—a serious step, especially when there are children, and when they may not have the gift of contented celibacy as did Paul. 2. Tell them to dwell under the same roof but not to cohabit as husband and wife—a strain which is beyond realization for most people. 3. Tell them to return to their first companions if still unmarried, when God's Word condemns such promiscuity. 4. Tell them that there is no hope for them, thus making remarriage an unpardonable sin. 5. Just pass such people by, because we prefer not to face up to such unpleasant problems. 6. Tell them to join some church which will accept such broken lives, a view which I regard as pharisaical pride, for why would we be entitled to pass on such people to "less perfect" churches? And if they cannot be saved in our church how can they be saved elsewhere? 7. Tell them that we will baptize them, but leave them hang in the air as far as membership in a local assembly of believers is concerned, a step utterly foreign to the teaching of the New Testament. 8. Tell them that we will take them in, provided they sit as drones and do nothing but attend church and take communion. Now it may be that it would be inadvisable to ordain such a remarried man to the ministry. But the more I think about the

21

problem, the less inclined I feel to attempt to circumscribe in detail how the Spirit of God may or may not use such broken vessels in His service. If a murderer like Saul can become the chief of the apostles, ought we not be cautious about too many restrictions?

There is probably lurking in many of our minds this annoying question: What if the other view should be correct, that to continue in a second marriage with a former companion still living, constitutes a continuing sin of adultery? Are we giving a false hope of heaven to people who arc all the while still walking on the broad road which leads to destruction? This is indeed a sobering question. But is it not presumptuous to pose such a question if God attests to His accepting such people by giving them the Holy Spirit and His blessed fruit, even as to us? Would not the Spirit of God mightily convict of sin any honest soul who daily sought His will while living in mortal sin? And if it were the case that continuing in the second marriage constituted adultery with fresh guilt in each marital embrace, would not God have put in His Word some such statement as the following: "Any one who lives in a second marriage with a former companion still living cannot be saved unless he breaks up the second marriage"?

If the question be asked, "Why then did God not put in His Word explicit provisions for the reception of divorced and remarried people into the body of Christ?" we may not be able to reply. We may not be able to understand His ways. Perhaps too detailed provisions for those breaking His laws would tempt people to violate them with presumption. For we want to be clear that *it is His will for people to live with one companion for life.*

Let us also labor and pray that the church of Christ may be able by faithful teaching to basically win the battle against this awful blight of broken homes in America, just as it won the battle against slavery. Human slavery is an awful sin and evil, but the early church clearly had in it both slave masters and bondslaves. It is possible that it also contained converted polygamists, for a bishop is to be the husband of one wife, although there are many possible interpretations of this command (not a polygamist, not a ladies' man, not a remarried man, not a bachelor, etc.).

The example of Ezra breaking up the marriages of Israelitish men with heathen wives does not furnish the church with a pattern to do the same, for Paul commands Christians to maintain the union with non-Christian companions in the hope of winning them to Christ. I Corinthians 7:16. And Peter also speaks of the hope of unsaved husbands being won by the behavior of their Christian wives. I Peter 3:1.

The question of whether adultery is a state or an act compares somewhat with the matter of being married to an unbeliever. Surely that is a state, not just an initial situation when the marriage began. And for a Christian to marry an unbeliever is clearly a sin by New Testament standards. Yet we recall at once the New Testament permission, yea even counsel, to continue such unions with non-Christians where the unbeliever is willing. Does this imply the right of divorced people to continue their unions even when sinfully contracted in the first place?

III. A POSSIBLE PROGRAM

Permit the explanation at the beginning of this last section that this is not the program of either Goshen College or the Indiana-Michigan Mennonite Conference. I am speaking only as a brother in the church. And with you I feel some anxiety before this question. And yet, dear brethren, ought we not have the God-given courage to attack this problem if we seek the face of God in humility and petition? God knows what we ought to do. God wants to give us the wisdom to ascertain His will. God will lead us if we want to be led. Let us therefore not become panicky or begin to think of divisions. If our church should feel led to return to the position of 1875 would that be an evidence that we are no longer wishing to follow the Word? And would we thereby cease to labor for the abolition of this awful sin of easy divorces and remarriages? God forbid! Just as the church can teach against murder, and yet welcome converted gangsters and criminals, so is there not a way out for those who find Him whose yoke is easy and whose burden is light?

Here are ten suggestions for your prayerful evaluation:

1. Let us labor to strengthen our own Christian homes. No longer can we assume that a Mennonite home never breaks up. Some do. The influence of the world is beginning to be slightly felt on this point among us. By God's grace let us conquer this camel of unbelief before it gets more than its nose into the tent. And we want more than an absence of divorce. We long for truly happy homes, where husbands, wives, and children feel secure in love. From such homes come strong personalities to serve Christ and fellowman.

2. We want to teach the rising generation the will of God, for courtship that is wise, pure, and Christian, and homes that are happy and sanctified. It is indeed asking much of young people to send them to secular high schools and colleges, where their associates are not of our faith, to maintain the faith of their fathers, and not to fall in love with someone not of the faith. May I therefore plead parenthetically for a stronger support of our church schools—not just for the strengthening of the schools, but

for the welfare of the future homes and the Christian lives of our sons and daughters?

3. Let us go out into society with full confidence that we have a Christ who is the full answer to the needs of men and women regardless of how they have lived in the past. Let us not feel that we have a Gospel which is adequate, except for those involved in such evils as divorce and remarriage. And let us not turn such converts over to other denominations. To do so is to make a mockery of evangelism and missions.

4. Let the church proclaim clearly before all men that it is the will of God for a man and wife to make a success of their home, to banish from the start any thought of divorce if everything is not rosy at all times, to exclude absolutely any thought of exchanging the present companion for one who is younger, richer, or more attractive. Such thoughts are of Satan and the flesh and need to be expelled by fasting and prayer if need be. By God's grace we can have happy homes.

5. When remarried people get converted, as we instruct them preparatory to baptism and church membership, we must point out carefully the teaching of God's Word on the permanence of marriage in the law of God. We ought to urge them to seek the leading of the Holy Spirit in this matter in their lives. He is a better Guide than we poor mortals.

6. We must teach our congregations the duty of fully forgiving, and warmly receiving into our fellowship, all penitent sinners who come to Jesus with their load of sin and guilt. This is no small matter. We cannot easily help some people to see that a stand maintained for two generations is perhaps in need of modification. But if this redemptive program is God's will, those who are spiritual

will be willing to think and pray through this problem; they will be teachable.

7. We must handle cases somewhat on their own merits. It will be best not to make an elaborate code to guide each bishop and congregation. Few cases will be identical. There will always be need of Holy Spirit guidance and assistance. This means that a certain amount of freedom must be given to individual bishops and congregations to deal with individual cases on their own merits in the light of God's Word and the leading of the Holy Spirit. And let us not minimize the ability of the Spirit to lead His people. For the sake of the unity of the congregation, however, it would seem best to have at least a 70 percent vote for the reception of a doubtful case.

8. When a remarried person is received into the fellowship of the church, let that be an occasion for wholesome instruction to the church on the dangers facing our homes, on the will of God that divorce and remarriage be avoided, and on the marvelous grace of God to this broken sinner or couple in yet calling them in His kingdom. If done in a right manner this will be a means of warning and strengthening many other homes, not of weakening them.

9. It would seem that it would also be advisable to ask the converts to confess before Christ and His church that they sinned in their divorce and in their remarriage, and now to pledge their lifelong faithfulness to each other in Christ. This also would contribute to the strengthening of the testimony of the church to the will of God for the home.

10. Finally, let us seek to see this question in its proper perspective. We are not throwing away our objections to divorce and remarriage. We are seeing more clearly every day the awful outcomes of these sins. This problem may not involve more than one congregation in ten in any

given decade unless it has an extremely active program of community evangelism (as it should). We are not ceasing to witness to the revealed will of God. Rather, we are magnifying His grace by offering salvation and church membership to those who are called of the Spirit to repentance and faith after having grievously sinned.

I close with a quotation from President Theodore D. Woolsey of about 1880: "The irreligious persons have connected themselves in marriage, one of whom had put away a wife or husband for an offense not recognized by the law of Christ as justifying divorce. They live for years together, and have a family. At length they become believers in Christ, and apply to the church for admission. In such an extreme case as this, shall the request be denied? Shall they be required to live apart afterward, until the former husband or wife of one of them shall die? We leave the settlement of this case to casuists, glad that it is rare, and only remarking that its peculiarity consists in the performance of important duties which cannot be performed when once the parties are separated." All we need to add here is that the problem is no longer rare, and that a church conference cannot do what the writer of an encyclopedia article can do: leave the problem to others.

Preparing this message was not by my own choice. With you I dread to face this question as far as being a fallible human being is concerned. I was asked to speak on this subject, and I have sought to present fairly the major issues involved. Let us discuss the issue calmly and humbly, seeking the mind of Christ who alone is the Lord of the church, avoiding harsh criticisms of one another where honest judgments differ, and I sincerely believe that God will then lead us. To Him be all the glory, world without end, Amen.

See also the article, "Divorce," by J. D. Graber in *The Mennonite Encyclopedia*, Vol. II, pp. 74-5; *The Complete Writings of Menno Simons*, pp. 1041-2.

THE AUTHOR

J. C. Wenger was born in 1910 at Honey Brook, Chester County, Pennsylvania. He was graduated from the Sellersville, Pa., High School in 1928 and from the Junior College Department of Eastern Mennonite School, Harrisonburg, Va., in 1931. He holds the BA degree from Goshen College, Goshen, Ind., the MA degree from the University of Michigan, and the ThD degree from the University of Zurich (Switzerland). In 1937 he married Ruth D. Detweiler, RN, of Telford, Pa. They have two sons and two daughters.

He was ordained deacon in 1943 at the North Goshen Mennonite Church, Goshen, Ind., and minister in 1944 in the same congregation. In 1951 he was ordained bishop at the Olive Mennonite Church, Jamestown, Ind. Since then he has served as minister and bishop in various congregations in the Indiana-Michigan Conference District.

He has served on the Goshen College faculty since 1938 where he is Professor of Historical Theology. He is a well-known author and lecturer on topics dealing with Mennonite history, theology, and church life.